Musings of a Sleepless Soul I

shawn ren owens

Pacific Publications

P.O. Box 441 Norfolk Island NSW 2899

Copyright © 2023 Shawn Ren Owens

Internal design @ SIDUS LLC

Cover design & Artwork © SIDUS LLC.

All rights reserved. The characters and events portrayed in this book are a product of the author's imagination or are used fictitiously. Any similarity to real persons, living or dead, business establishments, events, or locales is coincidental and not intended by the author.

No part of this book may be reproduced, or stored in a retrieval system, or transmitted in any form or by any means, electronic, mechanical, photocopying, recording, or otherwise, without express written permission of the publisher, except in the case of brief quotations embodied in critical articles or reviews. Any brand or product names used in this book are trademarks of their respective holders and are not associated with Pacific Publications. Printed in the United States of America

ISBN: 978-1-922936-22-6

This book of

dreams/messages/stories

contains contents and themes

that may be triggering or

difficult to some.

Please check more specific

content information at:

www.shawnrenowens.com

For Thea, the one who inspires me daily, and without whom I would not exist.

CONTENTS

Title Page

Copyright

Content Warning

Dedication

Letter from the Author   7

Part I   14

Part II   92

Part III   170

Acknowledgements   234

About the Author   239

Letter from the Author

In my journey of reaching out for resonance within the universe around me, messages came. Some came with dreams. Some came with meditation. Some may resonate with you, and some may not. This collection was written over a period of time, and the words in this book are simply an interpretation (my interpretation) of what I have experienced along my journey.

Musings of a Sleepless Soul I, is about navigating through life's wide range of experiences. Some raw and gritty truths, but also hope and optimism.

Now, as I look at past relationships and interactions, I am looking from a place of nonresistance, and am able to appreciate the experiences for what they were. I know the importance that each one had in shaping who I am and helping me to clearly understand what I want from life.

If you take nothing else away from this please take away, that connection to the wellbeing of source energy, shows us that we all have purpose, that we all have value, that we all are eternal, and worthy of the life that we desire.

During this time, I have also learned that there is never a right time or moment to release the words that are within you. It is important to put your work out there. Don't hesitate, or weeks turn into months and months turn into years.

Our creativity is not bound by human constraints such as time and space. They are simply tools to help us focus and bring our creations to life. Perfected or not. The world should participate in the thrill of experiencing your art.

Sometimes

The distance between falling asleep,
And waking, is great
Other times,
The distance is so infinitesimally minute
Sleep should be a time for the mind to relax
To stop all of life's momentum
Even if it's just temporarily

Those that have left this world

Running, towards the sound

Of chatter

Of life

Of excitement

Their messages of great magnitude

Of much value

Their vantage point, so great

Please continue to visit

In those places of dreams

Somewhere, in the distance

Somewhere between sleep and

awake

Part I

Wild Raw Things

Walk with me

Wild and raw things

A heart that's full and free

No worry or give

Embracing each moment

A fiery passion

As though it's the last

The wild and raw things

If You Must Fall

If you must fall

Fall down from the heavens

From far up above

And crash through the

starlight

That you are made of

Burn across the sky

And illuminate the night

Leaving behind a stream

Of wondrous debris and delight

If you must fall

Fall with no armor

So deeply in love

Making your life

The life you've dreamt of

Teach those and guide those

That are all around

There isn't a soul

That you don't astound

If you must fall

Fall into the beauty

That surrounds you on earth

Rest more, relax more

And know your infinite worth

Plant flowers and gardens

Deep down in the dirt

Untouched by the world

And all of its hurt

If you must fall

Fall knowing for certain

That you are the bravest of all

And release all of the burdens

That now seem so small

No amount of validation

Is necessary for peace

All one must do

Is simply release

Most days without you

Are heartbreakingly tough

Be assured, without doubt,

That you are so loved

Vast Emotions

The array of emotions

So vast and varied

Like a kaleidoscope

Each one so unique

To the others

Each one enhancing

The beauty and depth

Of the feelings and passions

There's joy

Pure and bright

Like a beam of sunshine

Lifting our spirits

Making everything fine

There's love

Soft and gentle

Like a warm summer breeze

Bringing happiness

And filling us with ease

There's anger

Hot and fierce

Like a raging inferno

Consuming us whole

Leaving us with zero

There's sadness

Heavy and deep

Like a rain cloud above

Bringing tears to our eyes

And filling us with love

So let us embrace

The array of emotions

For they are what make us

Voices That Came Before Us

The souls that came before us

Continue to whisper

Showing the way

The wind that rushes by

The rhythmic rain

Falling to the ground

The mind has the ability to

journey to and fro

Sometimes even completely

detaching

Coming to rest in a place

where light and darkness

converge

Timelessness exists

Entering vastness and

untethering from all that is

physically known

Be willing to listen and

listen closely

Voices of ones that traveled

long before

They are reaching out

Words echoing

Complex stories and intriguing tales

Be willing to listen for their whispers

Acknowledge their once desire

Their once hunger for life

Their deeds

Their shortcomings

Their defeats

And their triumphs

Allow them to send encouragement

Inspiration

And hope

Downstream

Letting go of resistance

Is a liberating force

It frees us from the chains

That hold us back

We don't have to fight

Against the flow of life

We can let go and trust

That everything will be

alright

It's time to let go

Of the fear and doubt

Embrace the present moment

And let go of the pout

We can't control everything

But we can control our thoughts

So let go of the resistance

And let the universe sort

It's time to surrender

And trust in the unknown

Let go of the struggle

And let your heart be shown

So take a deep breath in

And let it all out

Let go of resistance

And let your spirit shout

You are worthy and loved

And everything will be fine

Just let go of resistance

And you'll find peace of mind

Leap Forward

We were all there

Uncertainty filling the

surrounding air

Unable to be shaken

At times

On every person's face

Even seeping from some pores

Fear

It was a persistent low

vibration

That refused to yield

Inviting other low vibrations

To join in

To steamroll their way

Into every corner of every

home

Seeking its undue attention

We allowed it to grow and grow

Ravaging the world

Truth disrupted Twisted

Falsified

Looking back now

I realize this is how it had

to be

Bringing necessary wrongs to the surface

Demanding to be cleared out

Placing a mirror in front of the stage

Reflecting back all of the misunderstandings

And lighting the misunderstood

We're given a chance to address

And to correct

The opportunity to change course

To gain understanding

A new perspective

To educate

And be educated

Not to forget where we've been

Not to question where we're

going

But to remember who we are

And what we're going to do

with that

Going forward

We are no longer generations

Lost in space

We are awake

No More

There is no more deflecting

No not anymore

You cannot address your

concern

For the anger

For the outrage

For the pillaging

Looting and protesting

No

You cannot play the victim

anymore

Not without first reflecting

Not without first addressing

the reason for all of these

things

There is no more deflecting

No not anymore

Only accounting

Only ownership

Of what part you played

What part did you play

What side of history are you

on

Universal Secrets

The secrets of the universe

So vast and deep

Are hidden in the stars

Their mysteries we do keep

From galaxies far away

To the smallest particle of space

There's so much we have yet to learn

In this vast and boundless place

The secrets of the universe

Are locked away in time

But with each discovery made

We unlock a little more of its

shine

We search the night sky

For answers to our questions

But sometimes what we find

Are only mere suggestions

The secrets of the universe

Are infinite and grand

We'll never know it all

But we'll continue to try to

understand

So let us keep searching

For the mysteries of space

For the secrets of the

universe

Are waiting for us to embrace

Messages Replay

At night

I pray that I survive the next

dream

The next nightmare

The next message

My dreams get bizarre

Sleep is less by far

Unable to stay awake within

the walls of my mind

The nothingness invades the

inside of me

They wait for this moment

And hold my eyes closed Tight

Suffocating under the pressure

I can feel them now

I'm not afraid

Their words

Trapped inside my mind

Sometimes painfully insistent

and furious

Stories invading dreams

They must be told

Demand to be told

Each night I must choose a

different visitor

Only one from the sea of

figures

Tumbling down into the

darkness

I fear that I am losing myself

Unknowing what is truly me

anymore

Their words bleed in with mine

Am I me anymore

Am I the me that I know

because of them

I don't remember what silence

was like

Will you forget me

I am too lost

Unable to be saved

The world of fragile beings

tasting their own tears

Calling out for someone to

listen

The sun rises

Paralyzing silence and sorrow

all around

Dreams bleeding into

disappearing realities

Am I awake now

Celestial Beings

Celestial beings oh so bright
Shining down upon us every night
Guiding us through the darkest of days
Bringing us hope in endless ways
With wings so grand and a radiance divine
They seem to float upon the celestial spine

Their beauty is unmatched

Their love is so pure

They truly are the light the

hope and the seemingly cure

Some call them angels

some call them stars

But to me they are so much

more

They are the guardians of the

universe

They are the ones who never

waiver

So let us all give thanks to

these beings of light

For they guide us through the

darkest of nights

May they continue to shine

down upon us all

And forever be close on call

Earthly Goddess

She walks among the flowers

A goddess in disguise

Her beauty unearthly so bright

It blinds the mortal eyes

Her hair is autumn sunlight

Her skin a flawless sight

Her eyes like the stars above

shining

Her lips a rosy delight

She moves with grace and poise

An angel in the fray

Her touch a healing balm

Her smile a warm embrace

No mortal could compare

To her divine allure

She is an unearthly beauty

A creature to endure

Her presence fills the air

With love and joy and peace

She is a beacon of hope

A source of endless release

So if you ever see her

Take a subtle moment to admire

This unearthly beauty

Who sets the world on fire

Accidentally Becoming Me

Have you ever pondered

About how you became you

From the forming of your first

thoughts

To the releasing of your final

thoughts

How certain are you that

you're even real

Not merely made up

An exuberant character

Being created inside someone else's head
Shaped not by your surroundings or even by those surrounding you
But compiled from bits and pieces of everyone that your creator has ever met
Burrowing deeper into their subconscious
Until the two of you are indistinguishable from one another
Some of your smaller pieces

Some of their monumental

pieces

Their humor

Your rage

At what point do you become

aware of this

Begin to analyze every

instance

Figure out what made you - you

But now your not really even

you

Not anymore

Only versions of you

Created for everyone to see

The worst kind of danger

indeed

Versions of you that the world

wants to see

They must not wear thin

Reflections become unclear

And stay unclear

Bringing a brutal storm of

awareness

Afraid of what might dwell on

the outside

The mind unweaves

Life

Not how it was imagined to be

Long ago

In the beginning

Do we even like the us

The us we now are

Is this what it is to be free

Know that

Becoming aware gives the

control back

Know that

You are allowed to change

No one's permission is needed

Or even necessary

An Unemotional Hell

A statue made of stone

Emotions never once have shown

Stand tall and proud and still

But within feel nothing but chill

Unable to laugh or love or cry

For inside these feelings do not lie

Empty

Cold and numb

Unable to feel

Unable to succumb

To joy or sadness

To love or pain

An emotionless being without

any stain

A void

A blank canvas

A ghost

Living life without the most

Basic of human experiences

Emotions are mysteries Elusive

and reclusive

Stand here alone and

emotionless

A sense of emptiness and
hopelessness
For without emotions life is
nothing but a shell
A dull and monotonous
existence
A non-emotional hell

So I'll Wait

There is a quiet stillness in the cold fall wind
It's as if the weather itself knows our grief
The hard truth can't yet be spoken
And so I'll wait
The air quietly whispers 'soon' as it blows by me
Carrying the same promising message to you

Everything must be in place

And so I'll wait

Pain must be kept at bay

But is the wind simply being

kind

Taking this message between us

If so I'll wait

Or is the wind inherently

cruel by nature

Blowing by just to witness our

sadness

In the darkness it is so hard

to see

And so I'll wait

The thoughts of you are always

Don't let this consume you

Not even one part

I shall be patient

And so I'll wait

And so I'll wait

Expect Beauty

We stare at the stars

With no haste held to them

Allowing the sense of their

endlessness

We gaze at fields of flowers

Without disappointment

Each one gloriously praised

for its uniqueness

We start plants from seeds

Celebrating their growth

Nothing in our reality is of

flaw or consequence

Imagine

To look at people with this

much wonder

This much love

This much understanding and

patience

To have no desire to control

To allow them to evolve

To expect every wonderful

thing for them

All that they are meant to be

No preconceived notions of

what they should be

Hanging On

Within a shallow grave

No sun penetrating

Skin color fading as it runs

out of time

Cast the life away

The ground firm in place

Tell me it will all be ok

Stop touching the wound

Get out of the way

Stop screaming that name

I see you

Through the red in my eyes

Holding it together

Surviving the memories

Inside Out

Who hurt you

Molded you

Shaped you

Burrowed inside of your mind

Changed you

Left you

Came back

Convinced it was your fault

Everything was your fault

Toxicity

Seeping in

Spewed from the mouth

The mouth that is supposed to uplift

But instead twists and turns

Hate flows out

Pure negativity

A disease

Spreading like wildfire

Passed down through generations

Not anymore

Don't let them win

It must stop

It cannot continue

In passing, I see you

You're twisted - inside out

We are more alike than we both

think

Worthy

Establish your steadiness

Ahead of an unsteady

environment

Allowing to Tune into the

frequency of the solution

Know it's coming

Hope

Feel

Feel it all

Alive

Numb becomes weak

Eagerly scattering the pieces

They innocently look on

Despising any accomplishment

Build from it

Be on your way

Value is within everyone

Believe enough to risk

Awaken curiosity

Give energy

To form your faith

To form you

You deserve it all

You are not lost

Tune in to the vibrations

Of solitude and joy

Value you

Don't effort

Reveal the true you

Share your path

You are already worthy

Beauty Unbounds

Unbridled beauty

Wild and free

A sight to behold

A joy to see

Like a horse running through

fields of green

With a grace and power that

cannot be tamed

Your beauty knows no bounds

It flows through every inch

Every sound

It touches the soul

It lifts the heart

It's a force that sets you

apart

Unbridled beauty

A treasure to endure

A blessing beyond measure

It shines within

It radiates without

It's a beauty that can't be

denied with doubt

So let it run free

Let it be as it may

For in its raw form

It's truly at play

Embrace it

Honor it

Let it shine

For unbridled beauty is truly

divine

Women

So many women in the world

What is your world like

What do you find joy in

What have you let define you

What do you pretend is ok

Overlook

Downplay

What do you think about

Ponder

Let envelop you

Is this art

Beautiful observations

No

Not everything observed

Might count as beautiful

Everyone sees

A different view

Experiences all differently

Comes away

Differently

That is beautiful

Find Her Again

Drain the forever

Time disappears

Eternity burns away

Time will never stop

Lost will never be

We will just cease to be here

We destroyed it again

Begin again

Time to begin again

Better luck this next time

Never leaving their sides

Go as they go

Hoping to get it right

This time - Maybe

Trying to see the world

Through their eyes

Understand their pain

Experience their joy

Close to Heaven

Close to Hell

Floating somewhere between

Don't lose the way

Don't lose the fight

The ropes tightening

Reach and take her hand

Jump through the light

Fall to the world in a

different time

Back to an unrecognizable

world

It wasn't a sign

Walking away

Walking away

I hate the hate

Was coming back a mistake

Tell Me A Story

Are you still there

Unable to hear you

Are you still there

Unable to feel you

Are you still there

Please don't go

Tell me a story

A heartbreaker

Tell me a story

A gut wrenching one

Tell me a story

With soul and sweat and farewells

Tell me a story

Where goodbyes are real

You are gone

How do I forget you

The black cloud following me

You following

You were the favorite part of me

The part that I cannot bear to see

The part to amputate

Please just let me remain a

little longer

Leaving me in my misery

The street sign burning out

Where do I go now

Untethering from the world

Rising upward

Effortlessly experiencing

Energies released

Everyone cries differently

Tears are only one way

Heavenly

Heavenly bodies

Bright and bold

Shine down upon us from the sky

The stars

The sun

The moon

All told

Their stories etched across the night

The planets too

With orbits wide

Revolve around the burning sun

Each with its own unique pride

Their mysteries yet to be won

The comets

Swift and fleeting fast

Leave trails of light across

the sky

A fleeting glimpse

A moment's past

A beauty that we cannot deny

The galaxies

A cosmic tapestry

Weave together tales of
ancient time
Each one a shining history
Of worlds and wonders
All sublime
So let us gaze upon these
wonders
As they dance and twirl above
For in their light
Our hearts and minds
Are filled with boundless love

Falling

Coming back to the end again

But why

Exhausted and lost

Darkness finally falling apart

around

Abrupt

Light piercing through

Safe

Alive

Left in the light

Buried thoughts breaking

through for air

The walls begin

Springing forth

Upward

Closing in again

Beautiful anger

Boiling emptiness

Broken perfection

Darkness

But the performance goes on

Further into existence

The death coming into life

Dreams just out of reach

The sorrow, the anger

Push it down down down

To the depth

Like all of the others

Rushing rushing rushing

To fall in line

Bring the calm

Bring the peace

Bring the intensity

Hold them all together

Wait...

Who's in charge here

Stuck At 2AM

I've become stuck

Here

At 2am

It's 2AM

Somewhere in between my dreams

and waking

Next time

If you're here in them maybe

we can fly

It's 2AM

My heart is breaking

Come and find me

Make it all better

It's 2AM

Demons whisper in my head

They remind me that 2am is for
the loneliness to sit in

It's 2AM

I've grown empty and cold

My strength to fight is being
overtaken

It's 2AM

I have been swallowed up

I have fallen with no
intentions or plans

It's 2AM

Never trying or even wanting

to escape

I feel as though I am just a

few breaths away

It's 2AM

The end of sanity and the

beginning

Complete madness and insanity

It's 2AM

Is this what it feels like

Exhilarating and exhausting

Wonderfully mind numbing

The inability to sleep

It's 2AM

The words rain down steady

inside of my subconscious

All of the words meant for

someone that's not here

Sleep

Tortured with dreams of you

Only to wake and find that you

are not here

Journey With Me

Journey with me

Trust my soul

Journey with me

Soon I may need to go

Journey with me

My world here is you

Journey with me

All this time I knew

Journey with me

Don't hold me too tight

Journey with me

I'll protect you with all my might

Journey with me

The pressure hurts too much

Journey with me

The pain swells in my gut

Journey with me

I can't go through this again

Journey with me

My time here is at an end

Part II

Tell Me About Her

Tell me about her you say

I grasp for the right words;

the words don't exist

Not just the right words No

words

You see

She is the pain that makes a

poet write

She is the melody that drives

a musician to play

She is the drive that pushes a

soldier onward

She is the voice of reason

that makes one calm

She cannot be explained by

mere words

She is the thought behind all

of those words

She is the existence and she

is the beginning

She is the end of reasoning

When I'm asked

In the end

I have to say my favorite moment

I have to say my favorite experience

I have to say my favorite moment of time in this life

has to be her

Seeing her for the first time

Even if it wasn't nearly long enough

That instant breathtaking moment

Yes

That is my favorite

Warrior

Survivor for so long

Fought to escape

To get home

Now gone

A life cut short

A young journey

Abruptly ended

Before even given a chance

To really begin

Some claim they've seen her

Some say she's still alive

They see her face in the street

Wanting to believe

Swearing they catch a glimpse of her

But she's not here

Her restless spirit roams

Searching for answers

Searching for justice

Wondering why

Calling out to anyone that will listen

Anger growing with each passing day

Her body looks upward

Out of a watery grave

Waiting to be found

Yet no one has found her

Together

All the strong women I've

known

Have bettered me

By their presence

By being in my life

Honored to be born of a strong

woman

Although she did not get to

stay on this earth long

She instilled a lot

An understanding that we must

understand

A love and respect for

humanity

All of its diversity

celebrated

Not muted

We are all here together

In the same place

At the same time

For a reason

Together

Each individual tasked with an

important role

An essential role

Without you the whole is

weakened

Without you we are all

lessened

Make the difference that you

were brought here to make

Reflection

Last night, I sat in the crisp

still air.

Thoughts in my mind,

raced with fear.

With flair.

Listening to the music, left

over from the faded daylight.

Just me.

And the moon.

And the animals of night.

Sounds moved through the breeze. Guiding my soul. Whispering. Urging me. To now set my goals.

Who am I? Sometimes I think I know. I am made up of every life interaction. Every song, conversation, and show.

The future is near, upon me. Approaching closer every day.

I know that I must be patient.
To learn, and grow. My way.

What will I do to change the
world?
My world. Our world.

The possibilities are endless.
Daunting .
Others that lived before me,
looking down. Watching.

Seeing what I will do? Or
maybe how I will measure up?

Are they looking on with pressure? With expectation?

Or are they looking on with encouragement?
Guidance and assurance?

I would like to think the latter.

Playing the Role

A wild thing roams the land

With fur as dark as night

It prowls and stalks its prey

With all its might and fright

Its eyes are bright and fierce

Its teeth are sharp as knives

It roars and snarls and growls

As it lives its life

A creature of the forest

A beast of the wild

It lives by its own rules

It's free and undefiled

But do not fear this wild

thing

For it's a part of nature's

plan

It plays its role with grace

In this wild and vast land

Create

We are all characters

Of our own making

Working to find purpose in

life

Feeling an obligation to

create

Journeying to find the correct

path

Our spirituality

Our salvation

Hoping to fulfill a purpose

To make an impact in others lives

To be driven and considered of value

The past gives us strength

Observations and wisdom

Write them all down

They are magic

Every experience

Trial

Victory

Heartache

Write them all down

They are our story

Inspire others

Language is a beauty

That must be preserved

Weaving lyrics into a

beautiful melody

So that no one will hear the

despair

The dreamers

The writers

The singers

The poets

With the nonsense of life

Swirling and twirling

The world desperately needs
them right now
As it continues to crash all
around
Struggling so much
Thinking that it must make
sense
We must force it to make sense
Make it make sense
It seems like it's been a
lifetime
But life is only a moment
Beauty must come from this
hurt

If only we continue to create

Humans

Souls continued

Arriving together

Working to establish

steadiness

Ahead of an unsteady

environment

And in the end we were all

just human

Only human

Some messy

Some vain

Some brilliant

Some insane

Seeing such beauty

And wanting everything

Holding the world within their

grasps

Finding a reason to be

Not fully knowing in the

beginning

We teetered entirely on the

edge of existence

That we were the power as well

as the downfall

Of life

Of change

Of destruction

The power and the downfall -

of it all

We held the entire world

within our grasps

How dangerous it seems now to

truly know that

To fully understand that

Fully understand the power of

our creations

And To fully understand the

power of our destruction

Still at the end of it

We were all

Only humans

Attempting to be gods

Humans

Replaced by fools

Dream Thieves

Go to sleep

Leave this world

Leave

Seeing through

Looking searching

For the empty souls The

barterers of life

The stolen time will lead to

the stealers of time

Thieves

Avoid their eyes

Don't stay too long

You won't be able to leave

Leave

Thieves

Selling your dreams Dreams for

sale

Why must I stay behind

Holding on

Unravel here

Unravel there

Slipping loose

Pulled back in

Let me go

Surrounded by a place of

madness

There's no place like madness

Down a deep black hole

At the end of the road

Follow it through

All of the colors bleed

together

Then they dissipate

On the way down

Hold tight

They say

I want you to stay

But don't hesitate Leave

Don't stay

Feelings throughout Emotions

extinct

Unable to save myself

Unable to save anyone else

Don't tell me more

More than I need to know

Dreams for sale

Sell your dreams here

Not happy with your dream

Return for a full refund

Dreams for sale

Sell your dreams here

Defective dreams refurbished

Half off today only

Make them yours

Don't delay

Dreams for sale

Sell your dreams here

Untethering from the world

Rising upward Effortlessly

Energies released

I'm glad at least one of us

made it

Toxicity

Chasing perdition

Her blood stained hands

The Feel of Red

Demanding center stage

Passion

Tenderness

Rage

Encompassed between two souls

In need of space

Pounding blood coursing

through veins

How it does race

Wine and clothes spill to the floor

No conversation is in store

Slip away silently in the night

Or wait to abhor the morning light

Surfaces harder to hold on

Hands begin slipping away

Anger yelled

Tears all dried up inside

Done with wanting to stay

Not staying for another day

Burning and bleeding

Carrying on through the night

- Scared

Meeting morning

Disappointed

Unsure of what to do

Letting him back in the door

Sealing their fate

His blood stained hands

The Others

While entire species vanished

The others came

While humans' hated humans

The others came

While the world was hell bent

on destruction

The others came

While innocence got held

hostage

The others came

While demons danced around

with delight

The others came

The others came

The others came

To shine their light

To all who wished their may

And wished their might

The universe is wielding

what's right

The evil must yield their

plight

The others came

And they're ready to fight

Lacking

I overhear them talk

You can't manufacture emotions

I beg to differ however

I expected life to be

different

Not to find myself crumbling

At times I find myself failing

at it

Carrying a tremendous weight

Close to snapping

Lacking emotional

functionality

In order to process feelings

Then sickness

Being forced to slow down

Disappearing into the void of

the world

Just me

Becoming the silence The

solitude

Alignment

Tuning out the chatter of the

world

Listening to the inner

guidance

What is truly important

What is happiness

Who am I

Sometimes I think I know

Most Days I am more machine

Than human

And I am still discovering

How to be okay with that

After all it's not normal

To manufacture emotions

Confessions of a Human Robot

Not as other children were

Emotions I did lack

Unsure of what my life would be

Walls I began to stack

Fascinated by how others had them

And so effortlessly

It was an unobtainable gem

To know the depth of endless reflection

A daunting task for most to take on

A need to understand human direction

To grow and ask and ponder life

Obstacles and difficulties

This is not what I wish to strife

Unbecoming what others wanted

Will they stay

Will they go

In those moments

I was haunted

A glimpse into that thunderous tide

Grasping as the humanity leaves

All I know is that I tried

I tried to be like all the others

It was simply out of reach

Life

By admission

I did not want to be there

Sitting in the humid night air

Just me and the sky

And the insects of the night

Surrounded by the vibrations

of the earth

Energy swirling around

The moon

Encapsulated by feathery wisps

Previously lost on which way

to go

Now listening to their words

and knowing

There is always guidance along

the way

I understand now

All that pass by

All that hear these words

Take off the armor

Heavy and binding tight

Guarding against the world

There is no pressure

Enjoy this time without a fight

Experience the moment

Finding comfort in knowing

There can never be nothingness

Everywhere you look something is created

We are the creators

Looking toward the nothingness and creating

Yes at first I did not want to be there

But now I'm glad that I came

Answers in a Dream

What has been gained

What was inherited

Freedom? Or a trap

What is the point of it all

Wanting to be done

The winding path ahead

Unclear on where to go

Finding there's nowhere to go

No way out

Each person born to die

Who is right

Who is wrong

The lies stacking up

Discrepancies abound

Anger changing to grief

Feeling so helpless

All standing and waiting

For the cure to life

At the point of delirium

In which nothing makes sense

Yet strangely

Everything makes sense

How did we get it all so wrong

Feel confident enough

To run

Run

Run

Away from the mundane

Let the idea of imagination

Be so irresistible

Intoxicating even

Softly and subtly they whisper

What they really wish we knew

If we don't change now

Is that all of this will

indeed destroy you

Invasion of Sleep

I'm asleep

And yet somehow still awake

Is this me

I am much a part of this

entire production

Yet I am not

The scene plays out in front

of me

Strange and eerily familiar

Obscure of real people

standing before me

Instead there are only painted shapes and broad paint brush strokes

Different nights are different tales

Different people

Who are they

Will I remember this one in the morning

Yes I have trained my memory to do just that

Does it really matter though

I am no closer to piecing all these stories together

The conscious frustration

slowly driving me to madness

Soon minutes is a new day

A new day of little rest

A new day of little real sleep

The struggle

The invasion of my time

Of my rest

If only it made sense

Any of it made sense

If only I could feel that it

was all for something

For someone

Be Still

Manifesting power encircles

Creating worlds and expanding

the universe

Start again

We've created the good

We've created the bad

The scary

The evil

All that used to excite

All that used to intrigue

A breathtaking stare unable to look away

The other side of heartache

Through tears and loss and hate

The other side of heartache

Through darkness closing in

The other side of heartache

Days and weeks and months

The other side of heartache

You've made it back into the sun

Be still my mind

Focus on the goal

Be still my heart

All is not lost for now

Be still my patience

Not everyone has woke

Be still my life

More is yet to come

Bourbon and a Backhoe

Though she tried to be strong

She grabbed what was left of

her heart

Now shattered in her chest

A common tale told

Oblivious of it happening

Unable to handle

The once desire

Reducing

Discontinuing

Diluting one another

No one could provide a rewind button

It wouldn't have mattered much

She watched her dreams slowly slip away

What was once the exact reasons

For falling in love

Were now the reasons

They fell out

So much time wasted on him

Beautifully depressing and real

Now buried deep in the ground

The senseless endless feelings

now gone

The belong to have one another

She kept telling herself

As she turned off the ignition

and too another swallow

Able to make it through this

New territory

Nothing ever experienced

before

No one tells it's like being

willing to drown

No one tells it's like the

first deep breath

Breaking the surface of the water

Whatever it takes

We want everything

We say nothing

Why is it easier this way

Death Chatter

Listening carefully for a

sound

Only silence and stillness

abound

Distant at first and growing

sporadic

Small muffled beat one

Beat two

Beat three

Madness beginning within me

No it's all wrong

Where is the order

The pattern

The sanity

The structure and conformity

This is not how it was

supposed to be

Not at all

Patiently waiting for the

nightmare to begin

Waiting to see them

Waiting for the worst

There's no time for crying

There's no room for fear

Is this a debt being paid from the past

Unable to decipher what to do

Unable to completely hear

The night is full of muffled noise

There is no peace

There is no sleep

There is only an endless room of chatter

Indistinguishable chatter

Knowing too much

Not wanting to be this close

Souls Intertwined

Simply watching you cross a room

The world behind your eyes

Intriguingly draws me in

Our lives weaved together

Composed of space and time

In that moment my heart was no longer my own

Fear eroded by vulnerability

But worse having to leave

To say goodbye

Aware of the amount of time

that will pass

A word from your lips

A raise from your brow

A touch from your hand

Making the tough times

bearable

The thoughts of you are always

I couldn't image

Anyone else next to my skin

Longing to explore the story

of you

Realizing that every day does

matter

That tomorrow is truly never promised

And that a heart can break

It can even shatter

Life happens

In those little moments

In between decisions

Life

It starts to begin again

I shall be patient

Until I get to see you again

Faceless Boy

Steps from sleep

Becoming aware of the feeling

Associated with the thought

A few hours in

And a small boy appears

Of whom I do not know

Toddler age

Straight blonde hair

Yellow footed pajamas

Stained with dirt

Walking around

Crying

Lost

Faceless

He's unable to find anyone familiar

Unable to fit in and nowhere to go

Allowing others to see their pain

Is not for everyone

Loss is loss

No matter the circumstance

Specifics are not necessary

No feelings need to be
defended

It was a loss

Already gutted

Heart of stone

How to go on

The body must still process it

Allow it to be processed

But don't stay

Don't allow it to infiltrate
your core

Emotions

Tune into the frequency of the
solution

Know it's coming

Going into ketosis

Immerse into the solitude

Know that pain and trauma

Is real

No explanation necessary

The Art of Happy

Are you happy

Truly happy

No not truly anyway

But I like having hope

That one day I will be happy

Truly happy

And until then

I will reach for the best

Feeling thought that

I can muster up

Until I'm happy

Truly undoubtedly

Happy again

Manifesting Us

At one point

We all wanted the same thing

And so we decided

And we became

Us

Manifesting into reality

This place called earth

To experience all of the joy

Along with the contrast

Remembering that we carry

Gold dust in our pockets

But not knowing why

And watching in awe

As meteors trial in our eyes

But as with all other beings

Living here and now

We are subject to

The monumental act of

forgetting

That we have all been here

before

Back to the Sun

Pain is kept deep inside

Fighting

Clawing to get out

Memories must be forgotten

They cause tears to build

To well up inside

If the tears come

They may bring with them

The pain as well

And that just cannot happen

Remember on the other side

Of it all is hope

The other side of heartache

Through tears and loss and hate

The other side of heartache

Through darkness closing in

The other side of heartache

Days and weeks and months

The other side of heartache

You've made it back into the sun

Another World

A different time

A different space

A different feeling in this place

One of them stops me and explains

That I can't be there

No not there - there

But at this time - there

Not in this time

I argue

I state my case

I don't want to go back

To my time

To my space

The truth of the world

Of my world

Is that it's full of agendas

So many people

With so many agendas

The moment that you don't

Fit their agenda anymore

Are we disposable

Out of Your Control

Finding my way

Surrounded by darkness

Through the thick fog and

trees

I fall to my knees

I can't seem to get you out of

my head

Trust me

I have tried

Making it a point to invade my

dreams

I get it

I truly do

You were never mine

Not really

You loved tragedies

And couldn't handle

discovering

That you were the real tragedy

That couldn't seem to love

herself

So instead you projected

Onto everyone around

Relentlessly showing your

insecurity

Destroying others to feel

powerful

But my perception has changed

Becoming Aware of the feeling

Associated with the thought

Giving control to change

everything

Part III

Untamed Us

Wild things preserve

Their freedom at all cost

They roam and they swerve

Never tied to what's lost

Their hearts are untamed

Their spirits

Unbridled and wild

They roam through the land

Their stories

Yet to be compiled

They are a force of nature

Beautiful and fierce

They are creatures of wonder

A sight to pierce

So let the wild things roam

For they are a part of each of

us

What is Normal

Be easy on yourself

Be kind with others

All is alright

And all is good

We will get there

Maybe not together

Or at the same time

But we will get there

Before the need for haste

returns

And the mayhem of each day

My wish for you would be

To walk the earth Awakened

To breath and take it all in

To notice the others

Still asleep

See all of their hollow faces

Expressionless

Writing their sadness

Recording their observations

Wishing for them too

To wake up

Normal was not working

Normal is not worth getting

back to

Understand that what you know

Matters

People are listening

Born of a Misunderstanding

The pain passes my tolerance

I'm too weak to react though

To the hospital again

So exhausted from this life

This battle

I wonder what I was thinking

When I decided to drop down

To separate from the heavens

Why I would choose this

contrast

It seems sort of drastic

Doesn't it...seem drastic

Maybe my words got construed

Maybe all I said

Was that I wanted to be rare

Not to be confused

With being given a rare

disorder

Yes

That is what I'll decide to

believe

The universe must have simply

Misunderstood my words

Tree

I don't recall the beginning

My beginning

Deciding to come forth

Deciding to exist

To be

Falling through the air

I've come forth

From the heavens

From the stars

From the source

Energy and vibration

Focused

All coming from the same place

The universe

Our universe

Agreeing to live

Only to exist

For a small moment

Like a tree that has traveled

Through its seasons

Cycling back

To fall back to earth

Once again

Magic of Us

In the stillness of night

Surrounded by complete

darkness

A blank canvas

And so it begins Creation

The feeling of enchantment

And euphoric haze

Magic

Bursting forth and refusing to

yield

Calibrating to the surrounding energies

Whispering to all to come gather and see

Nothingness becoming everything

The midnight stardust coats the ground

As each star is carefully constructed

The nightfall whispers in awe

As it is now scattered with a plethora

Of dotted lights

Even it is speechless at

seeing

Such beauty

To the Person I Never Saw Coming

It's a different kind of hurt altogether

When the person meant so much to you

It was so close

Almost perfect

We were almost perfect

But I'm broken

Born broken

I have accepted that

As long as it's taken me

I have accepted it

You never could

To the person I never saw

coming

You no longer exist to me

Utter Feeling of Lost

The moments in life

That I've felt lost

Like really lost

Are the moments

That are the hardest

I am thankful for these times

It has always been these times

Of completely feeling lost

That I did my biggest growing

I no longer dread them

And have come to recognize

When they are beginning

Without these moments

I would not be me

Remain Rare

You are here for utmost purpose

You are vital

Be easy on yourself

Bask in the savory experiences

They surround you

Do something for your future self

For your future energy

Helping the great expansion of the universe

Know your immense importance

Never have any doubt

You are here at this

time-space

Living this experience

deliberately

Every word exchanged

interaction

Decisions made

Thoughts and ideas formed

They have all

And will all

Be impacted

In great degree

By your presence

You are more than important

Please remain rare

The Mighty River

You try to pull up from the water

It grasps that much harder

The current clings to skin and bone

Bruising and tearing

No match for nature

Trying to scream

To cry

Wriggling

Wrestling

Determined to break free

Free from the world

And free to try

No match for the river

Eventually letting go

Releasing to float to the top

Laying

Eyes closed

Peaceful

As if nothing

Had just occurred

Doubt

Notice the pathway as you

journey along

It is all important to note

What you saw

Smelt

Felt

Heard

Each season passes by

Methodically

You reflect back on the life

that you made

Wondering how much of it was truly based on observation
How many decisions were made because you applied those observations
Learned from those observations
Everything that you've been now leading up to this moment
Will it be allowed to continue methodically
Or will the future
The everything else
The unhinging of time

Drastically change how life itself is viewed

Is there anything all that important anyway

The familiar

The unimpressive landscape

What are you rushing back to

What are you scared of

Do you feel the quicksand of time

Slowly closing in on you

Unable to breath

In over your head

Is this really what we're here for

Are we simply making too much of all of this

Can the pathway really be made much simpler than this

I have to believe so

I would like to think so

Souls Divided

The whole world's grief

Out on display

For all to see

Such division amongst our

souls

Souls that agreed to be here

At this time

In this place

Together

What happened to us

On the journey here

The utter shock and disarray

Have we become so frivolous

with one another

Why let the contrast grow

Why let it alter our

relationship to life

Can we not turn full speed

Back

Remembering the beginning

Our eyes blazing with purpose

Moving forward with no

resistance

Not stuck on what was before

us

And creating what is ahead of us

No longer carrying around this hate and grief

Simply being us

Loving one another

Continuing to live

A Life Not Lived

Years of hate built up

Breaking loose

Rumbling the entire

surrounding ground

Spewing forth out into the

atmosphere

Covering the innocent

Blocking out the sun

The hope

The light

In affect

Creating a whole new

environment

Every life living

Having a different experience

And we lived

We survived

And it changed us

A line created

A line drawn

Life before

And life after

Tell me

Does your guilt ever feel

heavy

To the Observer

How does an observer learn to

communicate as well as they

observe

It's against everything

ingrained within the observer

That talking is

And always will be

Completely optional

The senseless need to open

ones mouth

Only to say nothing

Endless nothing

That's not communicating

When everyone is such a

stranger unto themselves

Needlessly attempting to

control everything around

Thinking that it is necessary

Or even possible

All of it feels like such a

foreign concept to think on

Part of me wants to agree with

the above

Part of me wants to scold and argue on the judgemental approach
Are great observers ever truly great communicators
Maybe we are supposed to live as an enigma
Cut from a different cloth for a reason
Meant to be this way
Exactly the way that we are
Or maybe those that are great observers see the true humanity

As it is

And not as it should be

Even if this information is
shared

No one will care

So why share a deep and great
observation

Or for that matter even share
that you're an observer

Who will really care

Who will listen to them and
their profound glimpses into
the abyss of this world

Wanting it to make sense

Needing it to make sense

Feeling like there is a need to explain

Feeling the societal pressure to be different

To conform to what everyone else is

Knowing the reflection is distorted by socially constructed views

On what is normal

My Favorite Things

I find comfort in the souls

that visit

Knowing that they care enough

To check in from time to time

Like the old familiar smell

Of smoke that brushes past

Often in the oddest times and

places

Hi grandpa

I miss and love you too

Keep traveling in when you can

The encouragement makes me know
Everything's going to be alright
Or visiting with my mom in a dream
Always in the house that I grew up in
My childhood home
That my extremely rational brain
Knows doesn't exist anymore
Torn down years ago

But it also knows not to dare wake me

Instead allowing the reunion to occur

Knowing that it gives me a sense of security

To be there

Safe

With her healthy

With her alive

Those are my favorite times

My favorite things

By far

Midnight Intruders

Awakened abruptly

Jumping to my feet

I peer around the room

Slowly wondering

Doubt beginning

It was only a dream

Again I begin to rest

What was that

It was much louder this time

A quick scurrying across the floor

Much more

Much more than before

Who's there

Nothing but the silence of the night

A small ticking from the clock

A soft meow from the cat

Almost as if frightened

Closing my eyes

Only for pretend

I will watch for them this time

I will catch them

A pull on my ear

Ouch! That hurt!

I've got them now

They scatter across the room

Tiny little beings running

alongside dark wispy shadows

You'll not get far!

I exclaim

I quickly chase the bunch

through hallways

Past stairs

Past windows

Walls

And doors

Out into the midnight air

They move fast

But so do I

To the edge of the garden

Through the trees

Branches slapping my skin

Arriving at a tunnel

This is not familiar

When did this appear

Into the tunnel I run

They mustn't get away

I wake to no intruders

No visitors

Gone as quickly as they came

But came for what

An End

Floating higher

Higher above

Pulled back

Dragged back to earth

This time

This place

This moment

Not escaping that easily

Here for this moment

On purpose

Help me find my way

Weakness falls away

So many beginnings

And so many endings

Glimpses into how it could all go

How everything around could end

But it wouldn't be the first time

Now would it

Humanity will survive

We will adapt

We will overcome

But what will suffer in the struggle

In the fight

What irreparable damage

We have already done

Already caused

What's left after all

The world remade over and over

The count starts over

The sign reads

It has been "0" days since our last accident

One of the Forgotten

Forgetting

It must be terrible

Then again

You don't know that it should

feel terrible

Being divided; Willingly

divided

But not by your choice

Knowing that you don't belong

here

Yet not understanding why

Be careful; your wings are showing

The light pulling you

The darkness pulling you

In the midst of a tug of war

All because of a choice

So sad

It wasn't even your choice

They know that you are unaware

Unaware of who you truly are

Unable to tell you

For fear of repercussion

For fear that the same may happen to them

To forget

To be part of the forgotten

Do I dare to tell them the

truth

That they were a byproduct

Of their own kinds war

If only I could

Slowing Down

Reality altered

Surroundings familiar

But not completely familiar

Things are strange

Out of place

Weirdly out of place

I'm awake

At least I think I'm awake

Some days I find

That it's so hard to be

present

In the moment

The now

But those tend to be the best

times

That lend themselves to the

calming

The unwinding

That leads to inspiration

I am thankful for those forced

times

Of being present

Of having to slow down

Whether it's listening to a

great playlist

Or listening to you sleep

To the Shadows

A shadow fell away today

Unlike any before it

The freeing breath of air

Quenched deep the hollows of

my soul

A lighter time ahead

Coming Back

This world

The urge to stay tethered is

hard

Out of the calm door

Into the madness we fall

Everything Works Out

When the road ahead seems long and steep
And the trials we face make us weep
We wonder if things will ever work out
If the future will be filled with doubt
But somehow it always seems to go

No matter how low the ebb and flow

Things always seem to work out in the end

We find our way and we start to mend

Maybe it's not always easy to see

But the path ahead is meant to be

The struggles we face are just a test

To make us stronger to do our best

So when you're feeling lost and alone

Just remember you're not on your own

There's a reason for everything that happens my friend

And somehow things always work out in the end

Who's Listening

Wander through the busy day

Wonder at the brilliant night

New voices reach your ears

deep inside

Divine messengers surrounded

by those not listening

Into another chaotic day

What is Change

Embrace the uncertainty

dawning over us

Playing intensely within their

games

Who will reject this

acceptance

It's always been this way

The Road Ahead

The bright road ahead

It stretches out before me

With possibilities

And endless potentiality

I stand at the fork

Not sure which way to go

But the road ahead

Beckons me to grow

I feel the sun on my face

The breeze in my hair

I take a deep breath

Ready to embrace life's flair

The journey ahead

And the adventures to come

I am excitedly ready

I am overcome

With a sense of purpose

A sense of pride

I step forward

Ready to ride

The bright road ahead

It calls out to me

I am finally ready

I am to be free

To explore and discover

To live my best life

I am ready to embrace

All the love plus all the

strife

All that comes my way

Met strength and grace

I am ready and strong

I am in this race

To live my best life

To embrace all that's true

The bright road ahead

It beckons me anew

The Hitchhiker

Walking the blank highway

Darkness is the only companion

Encompassing

Enveloping

Senses spilling out across the

pavement

Slipping on the stones beneath

the feet

Untied

Reality encapsulates

Pulling and emptying

Filling up again

Release the ties binding and

go on

Acknowledgments

I would like to thank the following individuals for their support and constant love and encouragement in my life...

My wife. My life. Sharing this life together is what true happiness is about. Being able to communicate so precisely, most times without any words spoken, is such a magnificent gift. You make a difference every day and matter so much to me! I love being a part of every day with you.

My kids, Gillian and Tristan. You two truly understand me and have been such a tremendous gift in my life. A part of me as a whole. Without you, life would be unimaginative, marginal and full of lackluster. I will love you always.

My sisters, Lindsey and Talea. My dad, Tim. Thank you for always helping me find joy, and allowing me to feel the security of always having family be there no matter what is needed.

For the three amazing women that have left this earth too soon to cancer.

<u>Dianna Dillinger Owens</u>, there are no words to describe the wonderful mom that you were, for the short ten years that I was able to live within the magical childhood that you created.

<u>Marsha Wallace Owens</u>, for the next twenty three years I was given a bonus mom that helped me grow and become who I am today. I am forever grateful and fortunate to have had you in my life. The best nana that has existed.

Susan Burton, for the short time that we knew each other, you were a steady support, rock, and cheerleader within my life. Your earthly presence is missed daily.

All of the friends and soul family that I've met along this journey, your constant encouragement and support means everything!

Abraham Hicks teachings. Esther and Jerry Hicks. Everyday I am learning and growing more in my own understanding of the world around me. This experience called life would not be nearly as fun or intentionally possible without

your knowledge and guidance.

About the Author

Shawn Ren Owens grew up in Texas and currently travels between California and Georgia with their spouse. They received a BS in banking finance and a BS in corporate finance in 2006 from Arkansas State University. They are part of the lgbtq+ community. In an attempt to seek out answers for their own clarity regarding their life events, they received a MA in Biblical and Theological

Studies in 2022 from Belhaven University.

You can find them @shawnrenowens on Facebook, Instagram, Tiktok, and Twitter.

Visit shawnrenowens.com

www.ingramcontent.com/pod-product-compliance
Lightning Source LLC
Chambersburg PA
CBHW030257100526
44590CB00012B/426